MODEL
COMMERCIAL VEHICLES

MODEL
COMMERCIAL
VEHICLES

Cecil Gibson

Consultant Editor—C. B. C. Lee

A Studio Book

The Viking Press · New York

Published in 1972 by THE VIKING PRESS, INC.
625 Madison Avenue, New York, N.Y. 10022

SBN 670-48245-5

Library of Congress catalog card number: 72-172071

Photography by Michael Langford

Printed and bound by C. Tinling & Co.
Prescot and London, England

CONTENTS

Dedicated to my many American collector-friends,
especially Ed Force and Clint Seeley

INTRODUCTION

THE COMMERCIAL VEHICLE

We had some trouble in finding a suitable title for this book, feeling that *Commercial Vehicles* sounds a little dull, even if the subject is far from dull. However, it was the only suitable title for a book about the very large number of machines on the roads today which carry goods rather than private passengers (in the case of buses, the passengers are considered as goods), and, as I hope to show, these vans, trucks, buses, tankers, etc. are extremely interesting to the student of design as well as to the collector of model cars.

Their history is a long one; indeed, the earliest recorded powered vehicle was not a private car but an artillery tractor, designed in France by Joseph Cugnot in 1765, and it is possible that the early German designers, Karl Benz and Gottlieb Daimler, saw their inventions originally as replacements for the railway carriage, powered with the lighter gasoline engine and free to run at will on the roads. Of the two, Daimler started with a small engine which could be attached to any sort of wheeled carriage, or even to boats (the original concept of a power-pack), which he later revised. Private car and van grew up together and gradually drew apart, the lighter and faster car coming to look very different from its heavier and slower goods-carrying counterpart. (Nowadays that process is reversed somewhat: many American utilities or ambulances are just as fast as passenger cars and look like station wagons.) In the future, too, we may expect to see as much development on, say, gas-turbine engines in big trucks as in cars. Most people are primarily interested in owning and driving a car of their own, and a large number are interested in the very narrow field of racing cars, but commercial vehicles play an important part in everyday life, and, with the increase in super highways and traffic volume, a larger proportion of our needs are supplied by this means every year.

The design of the private car is diverse enough, depending on many factors such as size, speed, luxury and number of seats demanded by the customer, but, up to the recent introduction of the Wankel rotor engine, most development took place along the lines of better suspension, brakes, tires, passenger safety, etc., with the transport of the driver the main factor in the designer's mind. But this complexity is nothing compared with the problems facing the commercial designer. As in the car, gasoline engines or gas-turbine engines are available as power sources, but a large proportion of the bigger trucks are Diesel powered, an additional choice for the designer to ponder. Long-distance tankers and freight trucks are often extremely heavy, and may be articulated, so a long chassis is needed, and multiple wheels are common. The cabs must be comfortable and big enough to live in on long journeys, even big enough for a second driver to sleep in, and there are problems of visibility to be solved. On top of these basic needs the designer has to consider the very specialized use of each class of vehicle. A fire engine must be fast but with the demands of comfort secondary to the needs of getting men and fire-fighting equipment on the scene. A bus has to let passengers in and out easily, and a van has to be loaded and unloaded with the least possible delay.

Luckily for the designer, speed is not so important, but in exchange he has to provide a reliable engine which is easily and quickly maintained, so that running costs are kept down. He has, in fact, at least twice as difficult a job as his private-car opposite number, and it is ironic that while Pinin-farina is rightly hailed as a brilliant designer of motor cars, and McLaren of racing cars, very few people outside the trade could name the designer of the latest A.E.C. bus or G.M.C. gas-turbine truck. Yet a great commercial genius has a doubly difficult job, and is worth twice as much to his employers.

The many problems and the many ways in which these problems are solved make for a great deal of the interest in the photographs in the second half of this book. Note, for instance, the number of different shapes of the tankers in Plate 2, and on the same page a little bit of history has been noted—when SHELL/B.P. changed their livery and painted their vehicles white and yellow, this was faithfully repeated in the model. The bright colors on this page, as on every page, provide much of the attractiveness of these models, which usually have a bright paint scheme with large decals advertising the firm's wares.

Collecting this type of miniature is by no means dull, indeed these models often form the main interest of the thematic collector, that is, the man who wants only models of a particular type, for example, buses, fire engines, etc. Most people, in fact, do develop a special interest inside the hobby, which is fortunate, as buying and housing thousands of models would be an impossible task. With their brighter and more vivid appearance, a collection of commercials looks very good on a shelf or a show-case.

THE HOBBY

Model-car collecting has nothing at all to do with the currently popular slot-racing hobby, although some of the slot models are well worth keeping. It is more properly a branch of toy collecting, and has been popular for many years in comparative obscurity, coming into prominence recently through the efforts of various writers and authors all over the world. An increasing number of devotees have realized that they are not alone in their hobby, and a number of clubs have sprung up, excellent magazines appear in many countries, and there is an increasing international correspondence and trading with fellow-collectors.

It is usually difficult to explain why one's particular hobby is so fascinating, and while it is easy enough for the outsider to understand why small boys play with toy cars, it is often far from easy to see why grown men get excited about a rare find. Rarity in itself is always interesting, but of course there is more to it than that, and many people have only currently obtainable models on their shelves.

It is fair to say that interest in the motor car is the first requirement, and interest in toys second, at least to begin with—some people go on to collect aeroplanes or boats, but usually the division is quite sharp. The man who is particularly fond of veteran cars or likes to watch motor racing will feel drawn to models of this type of car. Most collectors, in fact, specialize. Thematic collections are very common, and veteran cars and racing cars are probably the most popular, followed by military vehicles, and, in the commercial field, buses. Thus the hobby reflects the interest in the actual car, although, oddly enough, most military collectors are civilians. The question of size also comes into it: many people only collect the common 1/43 scale, some stick to the smaller 1/86–1/100 scale models, of which there are surprisingly many. The advantage of this scale is that many more models can be displayed if space is limited. On the other hand, some modern plastic kits are made in 1/8 scale, and comparatively fewer of these large models can be displayed. The more usual scales for kits are 1/25 or 1/32, both manageable scales.

There are many ways of limiting one's interest in order to control the storage problem. Many people will only collect die-cast models, which is a pity, as some of the newer plastic miniatures are extremely well done. One-country collections, as the name indicates, only contain models from a particular country, usually the collector's own (for obvious reasons it is easier to start and build up such a theme). The one-marque people only have models of one make of car, for example, Ford, Renault or Ferrari, although this leads to difficulties when, to take one example, Fiat took over Lancia. One-make fanciers are only interested in one toy factory, and if the factory has been turning out toys for many years, it is a life's work to collect all the issues in all the colors, with all the variations. Even a comparative newcomer like Matchbox has its adherents, who try to find all the many little casting and wheel-color varieties.

The position of the model car collector is analogous to that of the stamp collector, who only has the time, and possibly the money, to collect stamps of one or two countries, or is a thematic collector interested in flowers, or ships, or animals on stamps. The hobbies are curiously similar, with catalogues, dealers and a jargon of their own (we have stolen from the philatelists the use of 'mint' to describe a model), and most of the fun is obtained from corresponding and exchanging with other collectors. While all this sub-dividing seems artificial, it is very necessary considering the difficulty and expense incurred in tracing the rarer varieties in good condition. So even a small collection in a limited space can be interesting if it has some central theme or motif. At the other extreme, large collections, given sufficient exhibition space, can be equally fascinating in showing the entire output of a single factory (something the factories themselves rarely bother to do), or some thousands of model cars of all shapes and sizes. Some very big exhibitions have been staged by the French, Italian and Japanese clubs. In this country these are more often coincident with swap meets.

The choice for the collector is virtually endless, and this is one of the delights of the hobby; on the one hand it would be possible to display some 10,000 miniature cars, on the other the collector who decided he wanted to stick to 1/43 die-cast sports-racing Ferraris made by Solido of France, would have five cars. These are extreme examples, and the average collector is happily situated somewhere in between, corresponding and exchanging models with people of similar interests here and abroad. Unfortunately there is no permanent exhibition for the collector to visit in this country, and, although most of the important collectors will show their models, this makes for difficulties. The Perelman Museum, in Philadelphia, has acquired a good collection of older automotive toys.

THE MODEL CAR

The model is as old as the car itself; there is no record of the first one made, but the toy firms in Germany were manufacturing quite elaborate clock-work models at the turn of the century, and this was the common type for some considerable time, being used equally effectively by the Germans and later the French. They have survived better than smaller, more fragile, and easily discarded toys. These clockwork toys were quite large, 15 inches being a common length, and some much larger limosines were made. Except for early lithographic tinplate 'penny toys', solid 'lead-soldier' casting, and hollow 'slush-molding' of 'pot metal', the small model as we know it had to await the arrival of die-casting as a process, which came around the turn of the century in America, and which was developed extensively by 1925 by the Dowst Brothers Co. in Chicago. After World War II, European designs have become progressively more complicated, with windows, suspension, steering, chromed parts, etc., so that today the accent seems more on the special features than on the model. (It is only fair to say that this does not apply to the collectors' models from the French and Italian factories, in which realism is the first requirement.)

One of the most important milestones in the history of the model car was the appearance of plastic as a building material. This was first used (apart from some simple bakelite models before World War II) in America, where small parts such as wheels and lights were molded in plastic for wooden kits issued about 1949, and a few years later the first all-plastic polystyrene kits appeared and were an instant success. Nowadays there are virtually hundreds of plastic kits, and every new American car has its equivalent model in 1/24 scale available in the shops almost as soon as the car itself. Plastic is a very easy material to work, and endless variations can be built into these kits, which are beautifully molded, with chrome accessories and everything needed to build a perfect replica. Perfectly shaped body parts and wheels, steering wheels and headlights are ready-made, taking most of the drudgery out of modelling and leaving the constructor to concentrate on the finer details. Plastic model cars are just part of the plastics boom in which boats, aircraft, rockets, human figures, etc., are reproduced, and the use of polystyrene has completely transformed the model kit scene over the past 20 years.*

Having discussed the three principal model car materials, tinplate, cast metal and plastic, there remains a rather amorphous group, including scratch-built models, which are built entirely by the modeller, and the use of odd materials like paper, cardboard, wood (usually balsa wood) or pottery. And perhaps one should mention some of the nicest models of all, children's self-propelled cars made of strong metal and powered by the young driver via pedals and cranks. Some of the very early ones are very charming, and the classic example is the Type 52 Bugatti made before World War II and powered by an electric motor, of which, luckily, several examples have been preserved. Apparently before the War these could be hired on the promenades of Nice and Cannes, but now they are to be found preserved in museums or private collections.

* Car kits are commonly of vintage or veteran cars, racing cars, or current passenger cars. From the point of view of this book it is nice to report that the Americans are now producing first-class kits of heavy trucks.

MODEL CAR MANUFACTURE

There have always been cheap and simple toys and there always will be, but the complicated die-cast model car of today (and indeed the plastic kit as well) is extremely expensive to produce. The mold for one model costs many thousands of dollars to make, so that only by producing very large numbers of a particular model can the manufacturer make a profit. He has, therefore, to be convinced that the model has a chance of selling well not only in his own country but all over the world, and a great deal of thought goes into the production of a new model. Some makes of cars seem to be naturally good sellers in miniature, Ford for instance, or Ferrari; and Rolls Royce seems a natural choice (Lesney seem particularly attached to Rolls Royces, and always have one in their range), and there is an almost endless selection of veteran cars. New cars now appear at the European Motor Shows at the same time as the models appear in the shops, and in fact the toy manufacturer and the car manufacturer have worked together perhaps for a couple of years before the unveiling of the new models.

When a decision has been reached to produce a new model, the first step is to make accurate drawings, and either the actual manufacturer's drawings are used or, in the case of a vintage or a veteran car, the owner is approached and asked for permission to measure the car, and numerous photographs and sketches are made. Notes about the color of upholstery, the type of headlights, and any other special features are incorporated in these preliminary sketches, and finally a master drawing is made of the model, scaled up four or five times. From this a model is made in wood or metal, and the tool- and jig-makers discuss changes they wish to be incorporated. A true scale windshield frame may be too fragile and have to be strengthened, and other slight alterations to the true likeness have to be made. The next step is to decide what special features are to be incorporated in the model—opening doors, battery-operated lights, for instance—and to break down the complete model into its constituent parts—chassis, wheels, spring suspension, body, interior, windows, etc.

The tool-makers now take over; theirs is an extremely highly skilled job, as they have to translate the complete body in reverse in the mold, which is made of high-grade chrome steel—a difficult operation. Small details such as door handles and body lines are engraved in the steel, and at every stage trial castings are taken to ensure accuracy. The same sort of operation takes place for the plastic parts which make up the interior and the clear plastic for the windows, and twenty or more separate castings may be needed for a single model. So the whole process takes a considerable time; the time is well spent, as the completed mold may be responsible for producing hundreds of thousands or even several millions of castings. This is one reason manufacturers try to produce different versions from one casting, and why commercial models are favored, as a single casting can be used many times with different paint and decals to give different models—as in the Tekno Volkswagen and Taunus vans and the many versions of the Corgi Land Rover. Molds are often given 'face-lifts' and such minor changes can be incorporated when the actual car gets its own styling face-lift and a new radiator grille or similar minor change.

The molds are now fitted in the high-pressure injection-molding machines and production is ready to start. Many of these complicated machines are designed by the factories themselves, and Lesney especially seem to have had a genius for inventing new types of molding machinery. The bodies are cast in a zinc alloy, known as zamac (or, in England, mazak), and the ingots are melted down and metered amounts are injected under pressure into the steel dies, the process often being repeated hundreds of thousands of times. Before World War II the molds used to break sometimes (although this is very rare nowadays) and these faulty molds are mainly of interest to collectors (if a source of fury to the manufacturer), as they make for rarity in the finished article. The finished castings are then 'tumbled' in revolving barrels, which removes any sharp edges, and prepared for painting by being degreased and phosphated.

Painting is an automatic process, each separate casting being sprayed the appropriate color and then passed on a moving belt conveyor into an oven where the finish is baked on. Special machines are used to paint small areas, for example, silver-painted headlights (which are now uncommon, as lights are usually properly glazed), tail-lights, etc. The model can then be put together, and this is done by conveyor belts feeding the separate pieces to assemblers, usually women, who build up the completed car bit by bit, first the windows, then the interior, suspension and wheels, and finally the chassis, which is rivetted to the body. Final details such as decals are added, and each model is given a test run to see if it runs straight and true. It is then packed in its box and eventually finds its way into the toy-shops.

This is only half the story, of course; catalogues have to be designed and printed, boxes made, and storage undertaken before delivery to the wholesalers, so the complete factory is very large. Lesney's, for instance, have over 160 skilled tool-makers and about the same number of automatic die-casting machines producing 10,000 sets of accurate castings every day. Their plastic shop can produce 5 million small items every day, and they use 2,000 gallons of paint a week. Competition in the toy trade is fierce, so any factory has to be run on efficient lines and must keep ahead of the competition. When the American firm of Mattel entered the die-cast model field, their new low-friction wheels were introduced suddenly. This forced all the other manufacturers to introduce crash programs to offer the same feature on their own models.

Pressure die-casting has proved so successful when done on a big scale that the older tinplate toys have practically died out, the only alternatives being the cheaper plastic toys which often originate in Hong Kong. This is a pity, because although the tin toys were simple, they had their own charm, and a certain amount of sameness has now crept in to the model car world, though several larger pressed steel toys are still made in the U.S. and Japan.

A very similar process is used for plastic kits, with a complete model being carefully broken down into separate components which are as carefully re-assembled by the builder, with the addition of chromed parts in most kits, a very thin metallic layer being deposited on selected parts of the plastic tree in a vacuum. For the sake of completeness I should add that a small number of manufacturers offer metal kits to be built up rather like plastic kits, although these are comparatively expensive (Auto Kits & Wills Finecast in Britain, Hubley in America, Pocher in Italy). These are made in a slightly different way, and are rather difficult to build and somewhat tedious for a beginner, although the finished results are superb.

The plates which follow give some idea of the many different types of toy and model commercials available today as well as some which are, unfortunately, no longer to be found in the shops. The pictures show how colorful these little models are, and why they are so attractive to collectors. They also show something of the various materials used in their manu-facture. Most are die-cast in metal, ranging from the comparatively crude efforts of the 1930s to the highly sophisticated castings of today, when trucks are just as complicated as their smaller motor car model counter-parts—and often, indeed, more complicated. While die-casting is most popular today, other materials have been more common in the past, and one of the plates shows some tinplate models, while another is devoted to the larger plastic kits.

The plates show something of the history of the model car, but in addition they illustrate the history of the actual vehicles, with the early simple and rather square shapes giving way gradually to the bigger more powerful and streamlined trucks and vans of today. They show, too, the enormous differences that can exist between similar-use vehicles—the chunky London taxi and its more exotic Bermuda equivalent, the enor-mous American articulated trucks for long-distance use and the much smaller British vans are instances—and the various forms specialized commercial vehicles can take: the Brussels Fair trailer, the Fowler's showman's engine and the 1910 London bus are so different in size, shape and function that they hardly seem to belong to the same world.

THE MODELS

1 TINPLATE TOYS

Except for plastic kits, the majority of models illustrated in this book are made of metal alloy, and indeed most models on sale today are die-cast. We forget that this method is comparatively new and was only introduced in this century with any success. Models before that were almost invariably made of tinplate, as it is commonly called, the basic material being color-printed sheet metal bent and locked, soldered, or rivetted into place. This method was originally used in Germany at the beginning of the century, and later in France, and a great number of cheap toys were made all over Europe before World War II. For some reason these toys were not so popular after the war, and new methods have pushed them out of the limelight.

Some of the best models were made by Tri-ang under their Minic label. Those shown here are post-war, but their size, the simple methods of construction with bent-down metal tabs, and the clockwork motors are really pre-1939. A high standard of finish is typical of Minics, and the glossy reds and greens are most attractive. It should be remarked that the advertising is by applied decals, not direct printing on the metal.

These tinplate Minics were made to roughly the same scale, and well over a hundred types were produced, mainly commercial. With average careful use they should survive indefinitely, as sheet metal, unlike some impure die-cast alloys, does not suffer from age and will only disintegrate with rust. Some large German models from the nineteenth century can be found in collections almost as good as the day they were made.

From the examples shown, the fire engine and the ambulance are pleasant models, and the mechanical horse with Watney's barrel trailer is unusual. This sort of promotional advertising coachwork has become less popular recently, due possibly to the poor vision in these vehicles. As can be seen, Minics liked articulated vehicles, so should a Minic box be found in a shop it is as well to check that both parts of the vehicle are still in the box, and, equally important, that both parts are from the same vehicle, as they are often mixed after years of handling in a shop. The single-deck and double-decker buses are well finished, and are great favorites with collectors.

The firm later went on to produce plastic models and slot-racing cars, and the swing of fashion away from tinplate has made them unpopular with children, but they can still be found in some of the smaller shops and are well worth collecting.

2 PETROLEUM TANKERS

Basically a powerful tractor unit, a chassis, and a large container, these vehicles show a surprising variety of design, and are very attractive as a display, although the scales vary; the big tankers at the foot of the page weigh five or six times as much as the small ones at the top. Tankers have always been popular. The first ones were simple, with one color and often no advertising, but the oil companies came to prefer free advertising to this anonymity in the mid 1930s (see plate 3).

Top row: Toy manufacturers like making tankers because one casting can be painted in many different colors. The yellow Dinky Toy 'NATIONAL BENZOLE' tanker was first plain, then painted in four different versions of which this is one. Similarly the blue Mercury 'FINA' Viberti BC 5 is one of seven versions. The other vehicle is a Tekno Ford 'ESSO' tanker.

Second row: Marklin's 'BV-ARAL' is quite graceful compared with the hump-backed 'SHELL' Berliet from CIJ of France.

Third row: Two quite rare models—the Berliet articulated 'TOTAL' tractor and trailer came from a now-defunct French firm called J.R.D. and the Commer 'MOBILGAS' from a firm called Micro Models in Australia and New Zealand. The latter was a good casting, and appeared in 'SHELL' livery and even as a milk tanker. The use of the same casting for a milk container has been adopted in Britain by Corgi, whose Bedford 'MOBILGAS' was repainted white and blue (and later matte-green, when it was re-christened the U.S. Army tanker).

Fourth row: Two identical castings from Spot-On: the first version on the right appeared in about 1960. The vehicle is the Bedford 10-tonner with a 2,000-gallon tanker. The casting is a little crude, although the wheels and interior are good for the day. When Shell-B.P. used a new paint scheme for their fleet, the models were also repainted, and the yellow and white livery looks brighter. One of the problems for collectors is finding both versions of such models, as sometimes one of the versions only appeared in the shops for a very short time.

Fifth row: The Foden 14-ton 'MOBILGAS' tanker, by Dinky Toys, appeared in Britain in 1953 and is now a collectors' item. The other model is a monster from Spot-On, an A.E.C. Mammoth Major with 'SHELL-B.P.' markings. This twelve-wheeled vehicle looks massive, but is said to be 1/42 scale. The tank is plastic, the rest is die-cast metal. Spot-On no longer make models in this country, although the name is still to be found in New Zealand.

3 PRE-WAR DINKY TOYS

A selection of early and extremely rare Dinky Toys sold in Britain 1934–9. They come from the well-known collection of J. W. Hemley, who kindly lent them to us for photographing. Such models are now only found in specialist collections, and many are breaking up as the alloy begins to fail and split. Luckily, the earliest models as the 22 and first 28 series, are of lead, and endure indefinitely.

Top two rows: A selection from the forty or so little vans in the famous 28 series. There are three different castings: the first a square van ('PICKFORDS', second row) with a separate plated radiator, one of a set of twelve which appeared in 1934, among the first Dinkys made. A second casting ('CRAWFORD'S', 'VIROL', etc.) came out in 1935, with the same colors and lettering. These are always called Ford vans, as the radiator is almost certainly Ford. The third version was like the second but had an uglier criss-cross radiator ('KODAK', 'CASTROL', etc.). This appeared in 1939, and again used the same coloring—note the two 'CRAWFORD'S BISCUITS' vans on different shelves. The 'BENTALL'S' van is extremely rare, one of a comparatively small number made for the store for promotion. This little model is possibly the only survivor.

Third row: Four mechanical horses with trailer vans in the liveries of the four great railway companies which merged to form British Railways. The merger led to the use of a single paint-arrangement in place of the individual liveries of the companies, the brown and cream of the Great Western Railway being particularly attractive. A complete set in such good condition as these is rare.

Fourth row: Petroleum tankers. Much of the interest in older models lies in finding examples of commercial vehicles carrying the advertisements of firms which have long since died, as in the 'REDLINE-GLICO' tanker here. The first Dinky tankers were plain, then between 1936 and 1939 some of these vehicles in special colors added gaiety to model railway lay-outs. The 'SHELL-B.P.' tanker on the right is slightly earlier, as it has a tinplate stamped radiator.

Fifth row: A varied selection. The Royal Air Mail service car on the left is a relic of the days when air mail letters were posted in special boxes and collected by these fast little cars. The Thompson aircraft-refuelling tender in the middle is a model airfield accessory, and the Holland Coachcraft van on the right is a very rare model. In the back row are two covered wagons in unusually good condition.

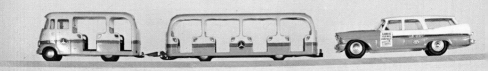

4 A MIXED BAG

Commercial vehicles exhibit great differences in shape and size, as their design demands are so different.

Top row: Tekno's Mercedes bus and trailer made for the 1958 Brussels World Fair. For some reason not many of these models were sold, and they are therefore quite rare. The other model is Corgi's Plymouth U.S. Mail car, which is an attractive way of collecting letters.

Second row: The outer models are both Corgis, the R.A.C. Radio Rescue Land Rover and the A.A. Bedford van. The center tow truck is from the Italian firm of Mercury, and, although produced in the 1950s, is almost pre-war in concept, later models being much more sophisticated with advertising decals on the sides, etc.

Third row: Left to right; a rare jeep station wagon by the Belgian firm of Gasquy; a simple but cheerful ice-cream van from the Czech firm of SMĔR; an articulated 'PICKFORDS' furniture van by Timpo Toys; and finally one of the most typical of British toys, a Dinky Royal Mail van. These vans in their distinctive scarlet and black and gold 'G.R.' motifs, were first sold in 1938, and continued, with minor changes, up to 1952, a long run for a single casting.

Fourth row: C.I.J.'s 'EVIAN' mineral-water truck. This, incidentally, fell off the shelf so often during photography that it is a wonder that any of the bottles are intact. Corgi's Karrier Bantam 'LUCOZADE' van is a simple delivery van, as is the blue Studebaker milk truck made by French Dinky Toys about 1950; on the right is an uncommon model by another French firm, P.R., the 'WATERMAN' publicity van.

Fifth row: The great French bicycle race, the Tour de France, attracts a number of specialist vehicles, mostly covered with advertising slogans, as is the Peugeot on the left with spare bicycles. There are no indentifying marks on the models and it is not known who makes them, but a great variety can be bought in France. The van next to it is a more prosaic British mobile shop by Corgi, but the yellow 'voiture balai' van is another from the Tour de France, the 'balai', or broom, of the title signifying that it brings up the end of the Tour procession and literally sweeps up the pieces. These vans carry a traditional broom at the back. The 'SAVON AMBRÉ LE CHAT' van, like the one immediately above it, is an advertising van by P.R., in this case advertising soap. Both these P.R. vans are now rare, and comprise the total range known from this maker.

5 MEDIUM VANS

It is an arguable point, but I have divided load-carrying vehicles into light, medium, and heavy trucks. Models of the middle size are popular in all countries and are built to a common scale usually, so that, as seen in here, an interesting exhibit can be built up. There is often an international flavor in this size, as the toy firms try to extend their markets. Tekno, the Danish firm, make many special models for Sweden and Holland, and some years ago sent models to America with English lettering replacing the original Danish.

Top row: These two Guy vans from Dinky were first issued some twenty years ago. They and the 'SPRATT'S' van below are part of a small series of Guys which do not usually survive in this condition. The rear doors open.

Second row: The other van is the Tekno 'ALLERS', advertising, I believe, a children's cartoon magazine from Sweden. The unit itself is a Volvo, and there is a difference between its long nose and the snub effect of the Guys.

Third row: In 1960 Mercury produced four trucks which had a simple metal chassis and a plastic top. Of these trans-European versions, this is designed to please Swiss collectors. The lettering along the sides is not done by decals but is embossed in the plastic. The Märklin tire van came out a few years earlier than the Italian truck and is of conventional manufacture, a one-piece die-casting with tinplate base. A neat little model, it has 'FIRESTONE' tire advertising on the side away from the camera.

Fourth row: A Tekno 'TUBORG' beer truck. This is a difficult bit of die-casting involving the use of an open body with inner plastic frame-work and sliding doors. The vehicle is a Mercedes LP 322. Next a DAF canvas-topped model from the Dutch firm of Lion Cars. This firm is remarkable in that it only produces DAF cars and trucks, and many of these are in plain colors. DAF commercials are common in the Low Countries and many of the models are exported from Holland to their neighbors. This model is well cast with an interesting radiator shape, but it is remarkable how bare it looks without advertising decals.

6 LIGHT VANS FROM DENMARK

All the models here are from one of my favorite manufacturers, Tekno. This firm has never copied other peoples' ideas, but produces its own answers to problems of design and the local market. It costs a lot of money to make a mold for a toy car, and smaller manufacturers often avoid this by using the same mold in different forms and with different paintwork. Tekno made large models before and just after World War II, and in the 1950s they began to make a very large series of small vans in various liveries to sell in Denmark and other Scandinavian countries. These were based either on the Volkswagen or the Ford Taunus chassis, and around a hundred have appeared so far, new models being added from time to time. The early ones are now unobtainable, and there were several made in small quantities only, so that Tekno vans can be rare, and are prized by collectors. Technically these models are interesting, because in the early vans the body is made in two pieces, one clipped on top of the other, and the whole rivetted to the chassis, making two-color paint much easier. The models have a high standard of paint and crisp, clear decals, and the treatment of wheels and tires is usually well done. The later Taunus vans have one-piece bodies and opening rear doors. Much of the fascination lies in the fact that few of us know Scandinavian languages and we can only guess at what the words mean, so it is perhaps better to touch lightly on individual models.

Top row: The Volkswagen demonstrator is presumably showing that the ride is so smooth that it is possible to stand on your head while being driven round.

Second row: The 'POLITIKEN' Taunus has an enlarged copy of the newspaper on its sides, and it can be read with the aid of a magnifying glass, a remarkable piece of decal-making.

Third row: The VW van on the left is an Express Delivery Service van made for the Swedish market and the yellow Taunus on the right is a postal van.

Fourth row: The 'AMSTEL' is fairly obviously a beer van, 'JYLLANDS-POSTEN' is a newspaper, I think, but the 'BUKO-OST' can only be deciphered again with the aid of a magnifying glass, when one can read that the product is cheese-spread with shrimps.

Fifth row: The model in the center is one of the earlier Volkswagens, an open pick-up. The wheels are simple, and there are no windows.

7 BRITISH LIGHT VANS

These vans from Dinky and Corgi are just as colorful as their continental counterparts, but, being commoner in stores here, we perhaps tend to underestimate them. They do not, in fact, reach the standards set by Tekno, but they are bright and well finished, with good decals. Apart from making a pleasing picture, these models demonstrate some of the problems confronting collectors.

Some models are rarer than others, because they were only issued in small numbers or were not reissued after the first batch. Such a van is the 'OXO' Trojan on the second row. Trojans are rarely seen on the roads any more, which gives an added interest, but this model, with the 'DUNLOP' and 'ESSO' on the top row and the 'CHIVERS' on the bottom row, made up a series of four issued by Dinky Toys between 1951 and 1953. Dinky Toys used a difficult numbering system in those days. For instance, the 'ESSO' van was 31a, but the number of new models being issued made this clumsy, so they substituted an all-digit system, renumbering 31a in 1955 so that catalogues of that date show the van as 450. Three vans were renumbered, but not the 'OXO', for some reason, so that it was only on sale for half the time that the rest of the series were, and is harder to find now. Just to add to the confusion, Dinkys issued two more Trojan vans in 1957, and these are also shown on this page ('CYDRAX' and 'BROOKE BOND TEA').

Other Dinky models are the Morris 10-cwt 'CAPSTAN', the Austin 'RALEIGH CYCLES', and the Bedford 'KODAK' and 'OVALTINE'. In 1956 Corgis brought out a series of cars and vans with the novelty (then) of having glazed windows. The blue 'DAILY EXPRESS' and the red 'K.L.G. PLUGS' directly below it are two such examples. Note the small but subtle differences between the Dinky 'OVALTINE' and the Corgi 'DAILY EXPRESS' next to it. The Corgi has definite changes in the windows, the casting lines are less crude and the wheels are spun aluminium rather than painted die-cast—not that this is an advantage from the collector's point of view.

An even more subtle difference is that between the two types of Corgi Bedford. It will be seen on the 'EVENING STANDARD' and perhaps more easily on the 'CORGI TOYS' van that the roof is ridged instead of plain and the radiator grille has been changed. These changes have been carried out in the mold, the rest of the van being untouched.

8 FOURGONS FRANCAIS

This is perhaps an unwise title, as I am uncertain of the difference between a 'camion', a 'camionette' and a 'fourgon', but the latter seems correct for a light van. These twelve could be spotted as French models even if they were stripped of their decals. An experienced collector can almost identify the country of origin blindfold by examining the way the model is constructed, how the body and baseplate are put together, the materials used for the wheels, etc. Most of these vans are taken from larger series, and some are quite rare.

Top row: The story of the firms that failed in the model car business is often more fascinating than the successes. The French firm of J.R.D. made a small series of 1/43 die-cast toys between 1958 and 1962 and then disappeared from the die-cast scene, which was a pity as their castings were good and most of the commercial vehicles were well done. These three little Citroen 2 c.v. vans are typically French with their corrugated roofs; reading from left to right, 'TOURING SECOURS' (roadside aid), 'AIR FRANCE' and a French postal van in an authentic shade of yellow.

Second row: Dinky Toys (France) made several models on this Citroen 1200 Kgm casting: this is the 'GERVAIS' ice cream van. The other two are rarities from the firm of Quiralu, a 'PRIMAGAZ' (bottled gas) and 'THOMPSON' radio and television van. This firm has also stopped making model cars now, and you would be extremely lucky to find them in a shop in France.

Third row: The center model is another French Dinky Citroen, but the outer two are the more interesting. The one on the left is a special promotional Citroen made for 'BRANDT' and issued under the C.I.J. label, although it is an identical casting to the model on the right, which is an 'ESSO' van by J.R.D. The explanation is that J.R.D. merged with C.I.J. towards the end of its life, and the latter firm used its castings. Promotional models like the 'BRANDT' are the bane of collectors' lives, as they are usually available in very limited quantities in one small area and are often out of circulation by the time it is realized that another new version has appeared.

Fourth row: Three C.I.J. Renault vans with rear opening doors. The center one is quite common (although its equivalent *Belgian* postal van is extremely rare), but the 'ASTRA' margarine and the 'TEINTURERIE' are quite difficult to find now.

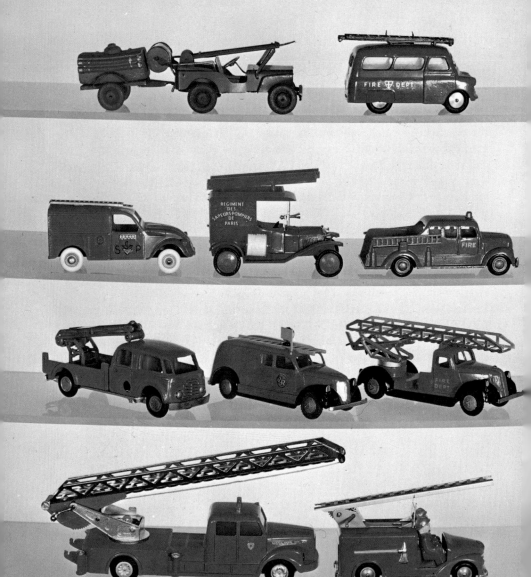

9 FIRE ENGINES

There is nothing so impressive as the sight of a fire engine, particularly if your house has caught fire. Their only fault is that they are all the same color. So, given that these models are all red and all carry a ladder somewhere, this page is an exercise in shape and differing functions.

Top row: The first model was made in France just after World War II, but I have not been able to trace the maker's name. It is fairly basic, a jeep with a ladder pulling a small trailer. The material is tinplate and the wheels are wooden. A clockwork motor with complicated gearing drives the jeep. Corgi's Bedford Fire Department van is much later, its motive power is an inertia engine, and it is one of the many versions of this casting.

Second row: The little J.R.D. Citroen looks good in red, again a multi-version casting (see plate 8). Next is another French model, a charming vintage Citroen by Safir, again in the livery of the Sapeurs-Pompiers of Paris. The chassis is metal and the body plastic. The model on the right is made by Micro Models of Australia and is fairly rare. Based on a Morris, this has an unusual shape, not seen in this country. Knowing Micro Models' accuracy I am sure this is an authentic miniature of the real thing. The ladders tucked in the sides are equally unusual.

Third row: Before they started making their beautiful 100 Series models, Solido of France produced a large range of relatively cruder models, of which this is one. These models often came in sets with two chassis and five bodies and an alternative clockwork motor drive. A Tekno with the inevitable Danish yellow flag is in the middle, and the model on the right comes from the same firm and is more complicated, with a simple two-position ladder.

Fourth row: It looks as if Tekno makes all the good fire engines, although this Scania-Vabis is a much more recent model and more sophisticated. It boasts tinted glass windows and a rotating escape with wind-up and extension mechanism. The C.I.J. is more of a toy and not nearly such a complicated casting, but I like it for its simplicity. It was issued in 1959.

10 BUSES

Bus collecting is a hobby within a hobby, and bus collectors are very often interested in nothing else. They have an enormous field to choose from, as there are hundreds of buses of all sizes and types. Many are most attractively colored and in such big models there is often room for special features like opening doors, stairs, and even drivers and conductors. Buses, too, are very typical of their countries of origin; one could never mistake a British double-decker for an American school bus or a French coach. Many of these models are available in a number of different liveries, and make an attractive picture on the shelf. They often evoke happy holiday memories.

Top row: The yellow American school bus is by Hubley, one of the few manufacturers in the States producing die-cast toys until recently: they also produce excellent metal kits. The casting is simple, but the shape is very individual. This model comes complete with a sheet of decals which I have left out in this case. The red vehicle is an Australian Micro Model single-decker G.M. passenger bus, modelled on the 1952 Bedford, a plain casting with no windows. Like all these Australian and New Zealand models, it is now quite rare.

Second row: Three double-deckers, all Dinkys. The one on the left is the Atlantean bus which came in several versions, the center one is the Routemaster bus with a short-lived decal which dates it as 1968, and the one on the right can be labelled with justice a model classic, as it is one of the many variants of a famous Dinky issue which was first seen before World War II and continued more or less unchanged up to 1963.

Third row: A French Dinky Autocar Isobloc and a French Solido trolleybus.

Fourth row: Left to right; the Hato bus is Japanese (by Diapet); the Dinky B.O.A.C. coach was a very popular toy in its day, and the sight-seeing bus is an interesting variant of the Budgie Motorway Express, repainted for the American market.

Fifth row: Two versions of Tekno's Volvo bus which comes in a dozen different guises as well as the savings bank version on the right, which has a slot in the roof. This was made for a Dutch bank.

Sixth row: This Berliet could only be French (by French Dinky). Moving the wheels in certain ways opens or shuts the side doors. The *nonpareil* of bus models.

11 FARM MACHINERY

Tractors, bulldozers, graders, etc. are popular with manufacturers, but one wonders if many are bought. Certainly they are now very colorful; gone are the days when tractors were either blue or orange, and the field is a wide one for specialist collectors. Here we have mixed farm and road-making machinery, and we have had to omit some of the larger and extremely complicated vehicles.

Top row: A crude but interesting ancestor; the make is Moko, later to become Moko-Lesney before Lesney started their mighty 'Matchbox' empire. The other is a very solid-looking model by Mercury of Italy, with steerable front wheels and clockwork motor.

Second row: A caterpillar bulldozer by Micro Models; a Weatherill hydraulic shovel from Lesney's King Size range; and another Lesney.

Third row: Part of a Mercury Massey-Ferguson farm equipment set. An interesting story concerns these Italian models, which were spotted by an American firm (luckily also called Mercury), and who bought the dies of the farm machinery to issue them in America. Unfortunately the factory burned down and the American castings are difficult to find. Next, a recent Corgi, a Ford 5000 fitted with Fen ditch-clearing gear. Lastly, a 1953 Dinky issue, the Field-Marshall tractor with its typical large chimney.

Fourth row: A Ferguson tractor by Micro Models, rather drab in its plain grey paint, a fairly good casting for its age, with good rubber tires. The smaller model in the middle is by Chad Valley, and is really more interesting for its box (not shown), which reveals that it was made under licence in South Africa. On the right a C.I.J. Renault. This was sold alone or as the basis of a number of sets of tankers, log carriers, etc.

Fifth row: Corgi always make good use of a single casting, and this Massey-Ferguson 65, here seen with a fork attachment, is one of several. The David Brown tractor by Dinky is from a later era, the colors are much gayer and the driver has a canopy.

Sixth row: This Fordson set is pre-war in concept if not in actual production. It is made by Britains, a firm famous for its farm and military models of all sorts. The scale is larger than usual, the driver is wearing breeches and leggings and a very pre-war hat, and most dating of all, his right arm swivels, as on toy soldiers. Britains have overcome the design problem of providing motive power in a narrow vehicle like a tractor by putting the clockwork motor in the middle trailer.

12 HEAVY METAL

Model cars vary in size enormously, and this difference in scales makes exhibiting a certain type difficult, as very small and very large cars look ridiculous when displayed together. So in choosing half a dozen or so models to demonstrate the theme of long-distance haulage a great many excellent models had to be omitted. However, there are so many firms making these models that a fairly wide selection could be made.

Top and fifth rows: The Americans are the people who make these perfectly enormous cross-country freighters, usually articulated multi-wheel vehicles with a wide, powerful tractor unit hauling a long box-like trailer with rear opening doors. But since the great days of Tootsietoys in the 1930s, American manufacturers showed little interest in die-cast toys, concentrating on their excellent plastic kits. In 1963 a small firm in Rochester, N.Y., Winross, began to make a few trucks, probably for promotion, but these were so well made that they were eventually sold to the public. Recently, the production has once again been limited to promotional uses and unavailable at retail. Both these models are by Winross and have identical rear-half castings. The tractor of the upper one is a White 5000, the 'HOWARD JOHNSON'S' is a White 9000. Unfortunately they are not generally available outside America.

Second row: The Dinky Leyland bare chassis on test with a 15-ton load is an original idea and a change from the normal sort of offering.

Third row: Dinky (France) is very good at big articulated trucks, and this Unic ten-wheeler carries tubes for use by the oil companies in the Sahara. It is a good casting with a single-girder type of trailer, painted sand color.

Fourth row: The Spot-On Austin Type 503 can be detached into two parts as the coupling gear works properly. The crate contains the Spot-On M.G.A. ready for export.

Sixth row: Two Foden eight-wheelers of a series started by Dinky Toys in 1952. Apart from the two types shown, Dinky made a wagon, a flat truck with tailboard, and tankers in various colors. The interesting point here is that Dinky re-worked the front part of the casting in 1955. The original plain, oblong radiator is seen on the left, while the truck with chains on the right has the second and much fancier Foden radiator.

13 ODDS AND ENDS

A page of models chosen for no particular theme except that I find them cheerful and interesting. In this connection it must be remembered that a collector looks for the unusual, the rare or the obsolete model rather than the latest chrome-plated issue.

Top row: Three taxis of varying design. The red and yellow Holden was produced by Micro Models of Australia, and is certainly bright enough. It came in sedan and police-car versions too, and is a model of the Holden of 1948. The center taxi is a very neat model from Corgi in the black color we are more accustomed to in Great Britain, while the one on the right is a Bermuda taxi, also from Corgi, a very dashing affair on a Ford Thunderbird body with a fringed canopy.

Second row: The Timpo 'HIS MASTER'S VOICE' van is so heavy and clumsy that it is quite appealing; it comes from the immediate post-war years. The Karrier 'PATATES FRITES' is a special-finish Corgi model for the Belgian market, and, like the 'TONIBELL' ice-cream van (by Spot-On), features a working occupant. The last model is more interesting: it is another special issue, one of several made by Dinky. The car is the Volkswagen, painted in the colors of the Swiss Postal Service.

Third row: The Dinky Conveyancer is an elegant version of a fork-lift truck. It has a number of features—the engine-cover lifts, the forks are elevated by a small key, and the steering wheel actuates the two rear wheels.

Fourth row: The outer two are by Corgi (the Commer 5-ton 'WALL'S' and the E.R.F. 44G 'MOORHOUSES'). Both are now obsolete, and they were among the first British commercial vehicle models to have windows. The 'KENWOOD' van in the center is Dinky's Ford Transit, a recent issue with many more features than the Corgis, which were ten years before it. It is a good casting with opening doors, suspension and a fully fitted interior.

Fifth row: The Spot-On 'SECURITY EXPRESS' is fitted out as a coin bank, with a slot in the roof. Another security van, the American 'BRINKS', is a slightly better model by Dinky, complete with two U.S. Treasury crates containing gold bullion. The center model is a highway tow truck in green and white 'TOP RANK' livery. It also comes in a different livery, red and white with 'AUTO SERVICES' markings; specialist Dinky collectors would want to have both versions.

14 LARGE PLASTIC KITS

Comparatively few plastic kits are models of commercial vehicles, although Airfix have made several veteran buses, and the Americans are now turning to some of their bigger trucks as subjects. However, these pictures show how effective these colorful models can be.

Top row: Airfix's 1910 A.E.C. B-Type London bus is possibly the most attractive model available at the present time. All the features of the original are present, from the open top deck to the artillery wheels. The driver sits outside (as do the upper passengers).

Second row: The car on the left is a dealer's promotional model, sent to car agents in America to give the customer an idea of the color and appearance of the latest cars. These models, which are often given away to customer's children, are produced by a number of firms; this 1960 Chevrolet El Camino pick-up is by S.M.P. These models are invariably in colored plastic. The other car is a police Lincoln. Airfix used the original M.P.C. molds and distributed this model in Britain. The police version is a glittering but sombre black, but the same kit can be used to make the gangster's version, full of secret caches of machine guns.

Third row: Jo-Han's Cadillac ambulance is very elegant indeed, and features opening hood and opening rear door with a well-equipped interior. This firm also produces a Cadillac hearse (which is not to everybody's taste, even if 'the last word' in model kits).

Fourth row: Aurora's American La France pumper is a beautiful model of a fire engine well known in the States. It has a multiplicity of highly chromed parts, but suffers from having slightly thin plastic, which transmits some light. However, it is easy to paint the body. AMT's 1934 Ford pick-up truck is from another American multi-purpose kit, made up in this case as a garage service car. The back of the original truck in these cases was cut away and furnished with a towing winch, spare tires, and other garage paraphernalia.

Fifth row: Another splendid Airfix model, a 1914 Dennis fire engine looking very spick and span in its City of Coventry livery. The rear escape comes off the vehicle, and the ladders can be extended. The neat detail of the pumping engine is rather obscured in this picture, but compare this model, which exposed its crew to the elements, with the all-enclosed La France pumper above. The kit comes complete with bearded and helmeted driver and firemen, but these have been left out here.

15 COMMERCIALS ON A SMALLER SCALE

Except for the bottom row, the models here are all Matchbox, either from Lesney's regular series or from their 'Models of Yesteryear'.

Top row: The big Fowler showman's engine has always been one of the most popular of the range, and comes in a variety of tiny casting and color differences which intrigue collectors. Although it is well painted, it responds to touching up with little dabs of paint to bring out the small details. This one is absolutely standard, however. The horse-drawn fire engine is another collectors' favorite, as it can be found in a number of different versions, with black or white horses. This is the Kent Fire Brigade version. One collector has reported more than half a dozen variants of the tiny foot-rest at the back, but this is really very specialized stuff!

Second row: It was difficult to know whether to include these in *Veteran and Vintage Cars* or in this book. The models are, left to right, the 1916 A.E.C. 'OSRAM' truck, the 1912 B-Type bus, the 1905 Sentinel steam wagon and the 1914 Leyland 'JACOBS' van. Note the wheel differences in all these models, with the front wheels usually smaller than the back ones—a tiny but important point.

Third row: Two forms of public transport; the 1907 Class 'E' London tram and the Routemaster bus of the 1960s.

Fourth row: The 'HOVERINGHAM' dump-truck is based on a Foden chassis; the fuel tanker is in an unusual livery, that of the 'ARAL' company. This eight-wheeled Leyland tanker is commonly found in England in the green and white 'B.P.' colors, and this Continental version is more sought after by collectors. The tan 'BEALES—BEALESONS' van is a rarity; produced in this special livery as a promotional model for the Bourne-mouth store, it appeared in small numbers and, as most of the models found their way into the hands of customers' small children, few survived in good condition. It was, of course, the intention that these little toys, based on a Pickfords moving van, should be used as playthings, but it makes life more intriguing for a collector.

Fifth row: From East Germany the firm of Espewe make a number of very good plastic models including this Tatra heavy-duty truck and trailer with steam-roller load. Until recently, models from Communist countries have usually been crude, but these are first-class.

16 RARE AMERICANA

American models of the 1930s have always been popular with collectors, and these models are now worth many times their original modest price.

Top row: This 1934 wrecker by Manoil is a rather fancy two-piece casting, and it is doubtful if it is based on a real truck. Manoils were one of the cheaper makes, and the wheels are wood with white rubber tires.

Second row: Two models by Tootsietoy, that on the left a simple one-piece casting of a Fageol Safety coach. Notice the ragged edges of the windows, which would never be tolerated today, and the one-piece wheels. These disc wheels are common on early Tootsietoys. The same wheels are seen on the next model, a Mack stake truck. This was produced in several versions, each with the same front casting but with different rear ends rivetted on—searchlight truck, anti-aircraft gun, etc. For its age, the casting is good. Notice the simulated chain drive to the rear wheels, which gives an indication of the era the toy comes from. An earlier variant, made from 1925–1927 lacked the 'M' monogram, door hardware, and the drive-chains.

Third and fourth rows: Every hobby has its classics, and in model-car collecting there are several classic series which all collectors try to find complete. Such is the famous Graham series by Tootsietoys, fifteen cars and commercial vehicles which are much sought after. All four commercial vehicles are shown here. The models were in such a bad state that they had to be dismantled, stripped of paint, repaired where necessary, and re-painted in the correct original colors. New radiator/headlight/bumper castings have replaced the broken originals, and new white rubber tires were put on the wheels. Normally collectors prefer original paintwork in their models, but in some cases such restoration is essential, although the model should be restored to as near its original state as possible.

Fifth row: The model on the right, a Tootsietoy Mack truck, shows how original paintwork can look after thirty years. Some paint is missing and the wheels are beginning to go hard and crack, but it was decided to leave this truck as it was found. It is of a date later than the one on the second row, as can be seen by its more modern lines and the fact that metal hubs with rubber tires have replaced the solid metal wheels of the earlier model. A second pair of dual rear wheels are missing from the axle holes, visible on this photo. The other model is not a Tootsietoy but comes from a simpler and earlier toy era, when many American toys were of cast iron in two halves rivetted together. This fire engine, with its bulky boiler at the back, is typical of the small cast iron toys of the period.

The selection of the models for the color plates was particularly difficult because of the enormous number of models available. Some of them are now rare and unobtainable, but many are currently on sale in Europe and America. Most of the plates have a special theme, for example, fire engines, fuel tankers, plastic kits, early American toys, etc., and the contrast lends interest, although the limitations set by having all the models of roughly the same scale restricted our choice.

The illustrations show a wide cross-section of the commercial vehicle in miniature and demonstrate how the designers of such vehicles come up with so many different answers to the problems facing them. There is no effort here, as in *Veteran and Vintage Cars,* to show the historical development of the commercial vehicle. We have simply photographed the models and let the shapes speak for themselves.

From light van to heavy freighter, each of these models is interesting to look at, brilliantly colored and decorated, and in most cases beautifully finished. Together they give some idea of why collecting such models is so popular.

GUIDE TO THE MODELS

The following models are shown in the color plates; the notes on country of origin, material and scale, are given for those who may find some of the names unfamiliar.

AIRFIX (GB) 1/24 plastic kit
A.M.T. (USA) 1/25 plastic kit
AURORA (USA) 1/25 plastic kit
BRITAINS (GB) 1/43 die-cast (and other scales)
BUDGIE (GB) 1/43 die-cast
CHAD VALLEY (GB) 1/43 die-cast
C.I.J. (France) 1/43 die-cast
CORGI (GB) 1/43 die-cast
DIAPET (Japan) 1/43 die-cast (and smaller scales)
DINKY TOYS (France) 1/43 die-cast
DINKY TOYS (GB) 1/43 die-cast
ESPEWE (East Germany) 1/90 plastic
GASQUY (Belgium) 1/43 die-cast
HUBLEY (USA) 1/60 die-cast, various scales, cast-iron
JO-HAN (USA) 1/25 plastic kit
J.R.D. (France) 1/43 die-cast
LESNEY *see* MATCHBOX
LION CAR (Holland) 1/43 die-cast
MANOIL (USA) 1/43 die-cast and slush-molded, various scales
MARKLIN (Germany) 1/43 die-cast (and other scales)
MATCHBOX (GB) 1/90 die-cast (and various scales)
MERCURY (Italy, re-issued USA) 1/50 die-cast (and other scales)
MICRO MODEL (Australia and New Zealand) 1/43 die-cast
MINIC (GB) 1/30 tinplate
MODEL PET (Japan) 1/43 die-cast
MOKO (GB) 1/43 die-cast
M.P.C. (USA) 1/25 plastic kit (re-issued under AIRFIX label)
P.R. (France) 1/43 die-cast
QUIRALU (France) 1/43 die-cast
RICO (Spain) 1/43 plastic
SAFIR (France) 1/43 plastic and die-cast
SMER (Czechoslovakia) 1/50 plastic
S.M.P. (USA) 1/25 plastic promotional models
SOLIDO (France) 1/43 die-cast

Spot-On (GB) 1/43 die-cast
Tekno (Denmark) 1/43 die-cast (and other scales)
Timpo (GB) 1/50 die-cast (and other scales)
Tootsietoy (USA) 1/50 die-cast
Tri-ang *see* Minic
Vilmer (Denmark) 1/50 die-cast (and other scales)
Winross (USA) 1/64 die-cast

INDEX

M

VW postal car, 42
  van, 28
Weatherill hydraulic shovel, 38
White articulated, 40
Molding, 14

P

Painting models, 14
Plastic as a material, 12
  kits, 15, 44
  use of, in kit-making, 12
Private car, development of,
  8

S

Self-propelled   cars,   children's,
  13

T

Tankers, gasoline or petrol, 20
Thematic collecting, 9
Tinplate models, 12, 18, 35

V

Vans, development of, 8
  light, 28, 30

W

Wheels, low-friction, 15
  plastic, in wood kits, 12
Wood kits, use of plastic in, 12

Z

Zamac, 14

ALSO AVAILABLE

MODEL VETERAN AND VINTAGE CARS Cecil Gibson
Dr Gibson is a lively and knowledgeable guide to the story of the
models of veteran and vintage cars *and* the originals they represent.
Beautifully made and painted, and accurate to the last detail, such
models have become collectors' items, faithfully mirroring the simple
mechanism of the veteran cars, the stateliness of the Edwardians and
the tremendous technical advances made during the vintage decade
after World War I. The whole history of motoring is here available
in miniature in superb color plates.